My GOD BRING YOU THE
PEACE AND COMFORT OF HIS
DIVINE LOVE

Michael

WALKING
THROUGH THE
WATERS

NANCY REGENSBURGER

WALKING THROUGH THE WATERS

Biblical Reflections for Families of Cancer Patients

With Discussion Questions
for Reflection or Group Discussion

UPPER
ROOM BOOKS®
NASHVILLE

Cover and interior design: Bruce Gore
Cover photograph: Robin Conover
Interior calligraphy: Suellyn Bielski
First Printing: 2001

Library of Congress Cataloging-in-Publication Data
Regensburger, Nancy, 1935–
    Walking through the waters: biblical reflections for families of cancer patients/by Nancy Regensburger.
        p. cm.
    ISBN 0-8358-0934-X
        1. Caregivers--Religious life. 2. Cancer--Patients--Family relationships.
3. Cancer--Religious aspects--Christianity. 4. Consolation--Biblical teaching. I. Title.

BV4910.9.R442001
248.8'6196994—dc21

00-043493

Printed in the United States of America

TO DICK
My dear husband,
with whom I walked
through the waters

Contents

Acknowledgments

Thanks to Suellyn Bielski, my next-door neighbor, morning walking partner, and friend, for her artistic illumination of these marvelous ancient texts. The beauty of her work highlights our true source of consolation—the healing Word of God.

Thanks to my friend, Susan White, who patiently listened to every detail of this illness. She helped me process feelings, clarify ideas, integrate scripture, and rework sections of my manuscript. Sue appears in chapter 2.

Thanks also to the members of the Christian Writers Group of Vassar Presbyterian Church for their critique of sections of my manuscript. Their confidence and prayers helped nurture my story into print.

Introduction

A STRAND OF HOPE runs through this book. It is written for others like myself—family and close friends of cancer patients. The reflections are based upon my journal, kept during the diagnosis and treatment of my husband's Hodgkin's disease, a form of lymphoma, cancer of the lymph system.

The book is upbeat, because after a few terrible months, things began to go well. Dick's diagnosis of Hodgkin's meant he had a very treatable disease. Chemotherapy and radiation treatments brought minimal side effects. Shortly after treatment began, his pain disappeared; his weight, after a thirty-five-pound loss, gradually came up to normal; and energy returned. The nurses proved charming, the doctors competent and compassionate, and the insurance company dutifully paid the bills. Two years after diagnosis, Dick's CT scan showed no enlarged lymph nodes.

I do not intend to apologize for a hopeful book. However, I recognize not every family living with cancer will experience positive outcomes. Some persons may go through periods of spiritual desolation, when God seems absent and prayer impossible. They may need to cope with loss of focus and even of function. All exists as darkness and pain. At such times, images and intellectual concepts may give no comfort at all. One can only cry out with the psalmist, "O God, why do you hide your face?" I personally did not feel such desolation, so I did not try to write about it. Spiritual desolation and its accompanying doubts do not reflect a loss of faith but are powerful expressions of it. Because of one's faith, the eclipse of God is felt terribly.

Although Dick did not die, I attempted to come to terms with death when it loomed as a real and immediate possibility. I grasped on to biblical images that comforted me then. I wrote from where I stood, which is all I could do. But I am not mourning the loss of my loved one, and I would not presume to speak to or for such persons. Healing from grief requires a different process.

Dick and I both remain forever changed by his illness. When he goes to the hospital for a periodic CT scan, I am reminded that the cloud of cancer will hang over us for a long time.

It was not easy for an introvert like me to share such intimate details of our lives. I am compelled by the hope that the story of our walk may prove helpful to others.

Do not fear,
for I have redeemed you;
I have called you by name,

YOU
ARE
MINE.

When you pass
through the waters,
I will be with you;
and through the rivers,
they shall not overwhelm you...
For I am the Lord your God,
The Holy One of Israel,
your Savior.

Isaiah 43:1-2, 3

PART I

Walking through the Waters of Illness

SAVE ME, O GOD!

for the waters
have come up to my neck.
I sink in deep mire,
Where there is no foothold;
I have come into deep waters,
and the flood sweeps over me.
I am weary with my crying;
my throat is parched.
My eyes grow dim
with waiting for my GOD.

Psalm 69: 1-3

1

Threatening Waters

FIRST COMES THE TRAUMA, the shock of diagnosis. It's cancer, the big C word. It feels like the ground is dissolving under our feet. Footholds give way, the water keeps rising, we feel like we are drowning. The psalmist uses this metaphor to describe his crisis.

Water can be black, cold, and mysterious. We are not sure what lurks beneath the surface. In the ancient Near East, people feared water. In the Old Testament period, frequent floods occurred when the Tigris and Euphrates Rivers overflowed their banks each spring. The Sea of Galilee could turn from a quiet lake into an angry white-capped sea in moments. The Mediterranean stretched beyond vision with no seeming end.

The sea was perceived as chaos and associated with disorder, evil, death. God was goodness and life, holding the power to bring order out of chaos. The chaos could happen in nature, but it could also happen in the lives of people: within their bodies, in their minds, within families, communities, and the nation. The writer of the psalm is not literally drowning. He is sinking in the chaos of life.

Serious illness can bring chaos to the individual as well as the family. It may feel like swirling waters pulling us down. Illness takes over, and the struggle for survival is all that matters. In such times, it becomes important to identify the real source of chaos. It may be the illness itself, or it may be related problems, such as inordinate fears, lack of support from a family member, inadequate finances, feelings of loneliness, inappropriate guilt, alienation from God.

19

The bad news is God never says we will not need to walk through the waters. The good news is God promises the rivers will not overwhelm and God will be with us.

> Do not fear, [*your name*], for I have redeemed you;
> I have called you by name, and you are mine.
> When you pass through the waters,
> I will be with you;
> and through the rivers,
> they shall not overwhelm you.
> For I am the Lord your God,
> the Holy One of Israel, your Savior.
>
> —*Isaiah 43:1-3*

God is trustworthy and God's promises are true. Claim them in difficult times! The text of a favorite hymn, "How Firm a Foundation," acknowledges those promises.

HOW FIRM A FOUNDATION

(stanzas 2, 3, 5)
Fear not, I am with thee, O be not dismayed,
For I am thy God and will still give thee aid;
I'll strengthen and help thee, and cause thee to stand
upheld by my righteous, omnipotent hand.

When through the deep waters I call thee to go,
the rivers of sorrow shall not thee overflow;
for I will be with thee, thy troubles to bless,
and sanctify to thee thy deepest distress.

The soul that on Jesus still leans for repose,
I will not, I will not desert to its foes;
that soul, though all hell should endeavor to shake,
I'll never, no, never, no, never forsake.

— *"K" in John Rippon's* A Selection of Hymns, 1787

For Group Discussion or Personal Reflection

1. Tell about a time you had a frightening experience with water. Perhaps it was a near-drowning or a boating mishap. How has this affected the way you feel about water?

2. Is being caught in threatening waters a fitting image to describe how you feel about the illness of your loved one? Explain. Have your feelings changed as you have moved from diagnosis to treatment? from treatment to cure? If threatening waters are not an appropriate image, try to describe your feelings using another image.

   Option: Using art supplies, draw a picture of how you feel, using either water or your own image.

3. Have you experienced feelings of chaos during your loved one's illness? Are these feelings caused by the illness itself or related problems, such as inordinate fears, lack of support from a family member, inadequate finances, sense of loneliness, inappropriate guilt, alienation from God? Explain.

4. Review the words of the hymn "How Firm a Foundation." Which phrase or stanza offers the most encouragement for you? Explain. Memorize that verse and repeat or sing it in the coming days.

5. What would it take to bring order and peace back into your life? Who or what might help in this process? What is one first step you could take toward order and peace?

6. Do you believe God has the power to bring peace out of chaos? How might you become more open to that power?

Then Jesus went with them to a place called Gethsemane; and he said to his disciples

"Sit here while I go over and pray."

He took with him Peter and the two sons of Zebedee, and began to be grieved and agitated. Then he said to them,

"I am deeply grieved, even to death; remain here, and stay awake with me . . ."

Then he came to the disciples and found them sleeping; and he said to Peter,

"So, you could not stay awake with me for one hour?"

Matthew 26:36-38, 40

2

Watching and Waiting

I CAME HOME from a meeting and found my husband sitting quietly in a darkened living room. The news he shared was a shock. After many weeks of tests, our doctor had phoned my husband at work that morning to say he had received the results of his abdominal CT scan.

"I think you'd better come to my office as soon as possible, so I can explain it to you," the doctor had said. In the office, he explained that the tests showed enlarged lymph nodes in the abdominal area, strongly indicating the presence of a form of lymphoma (cancer of the lymph system). My husband displayed extraordinary strength by going back to work and finishing the day after hearing this news.

Because his enlarged lymph nodes were deep in the back of the abdominal area, biopsy surgery was required to diagnose the type of lymphoma. There are about twenty forms of lymphoma, some extremely life threatening. Accurate diagnosis is important for proper treatment. We made the decision to travel to the Medical Center of the University of Michigan, about ninety miles away, for the diagnostic process.

Almost a month passed before the biopsy surgery was even scheduled. During that time my husband's health deteriorated considerably. He could summon no strength to go anywhere or do anything, he was plagued with intense night sweats, and his tumors began to push on other organs, causing cramps and loss of appetite. For me, waiting for the hospital to schedule surgery was stressful beyond words. My nerves became frayed, and at times I nearly panicked.

When the date for surgery was finally set, people told me I needed someone to wait with me on that day. Since it was to occur at some distance from home, I turned down offers from folks nearby. Also, I needed a person with whom I could talk about anything. One never knows what developments will occur during surgeries. One of my best friends, Sue, lives in the area where we would go for the surgery. We graduated from seminary together, share spiritual journeys, family problems, continuing education classes at summer school, as well as winter ski trips with our husbands. She would be my companion. To watch and wait with someone requires a solid friendship. Such were the ones Jesus chose to be with him in his hour of need.

My husband and I arrived early at the hospital on a foggy, dreary morning. We were told to be there at 7:00 A.M. for an 8:30 A.M. surgery. We sat in the waiting room in silence as others began to arrive and wait also. A developmentally disabled young woman came in with a caregiver. She kept crying out, "Peace and quiet," and her agitation grated on my nerves. Then I felt guilty for being so absorbed in my own anxieties. While my fears caused an oppressive heaviness, I did recall close friends whose prayers I had solicited for this particular hour. I felt confident the power of their prayers would affect our spirits—and the outcome of the diagnostic surgery.

Slowly names were called. At last ours came up and I followed my husband to the pre-op surgery area. A flurry of activity followed. During that short busy period, I met the assistant anesthesiologist, the head anesthesiologist, the surgical nurse, and the surgeon. The nurse explained that the four of them would be with my husband during the whole period of surgery. It was as if they were saying, "Don't worry, we'll be there for him." Meeting these people was reassuring to me.

About a week and a half previously, my husband and I had shared a consultation with the surgeon, an attractive young man. When he appeared in the pre-op area that morning, I thought he had the face of an angel. He explained again that if he could not get adequate biopsy material by laparoscopy, he would do full surgery. Laparoscopy would take about an hour and a half; full surgery, longer. He assured me he would come and report to me when the surgery was completed. He seemed very kind. I have thanked God through this whole ordeal for men and women in the medical profession who studied and practiced for many years in order to deliver such expert care to those of us who face fearful illnesses.

When I left the pre-op area I walked back into the waiting room and there was my friend Sue. We agreed to go to the cafeteria for breakfast. During the meal I talked a lot: details of the doctors' reports, my husband's optimism, frustrations with waiting for surgery, my own fears, on and on. She had heard it all on the telephone before. Watching and waiting requires active presence, openness, and the ability to listen nonjudgmentally. Sue did all that very well.

We returned to the family waiting room where I relaxed enough to ask Sue about her own family and daily life. About 10:30, the desk attendant called for me, I grabbed Sue, and we met the surgeon in a private room. He said the surgery had gone well, he got an adequate sample for the biopsy, it was a lymphoma, and the pathology report and diagnosis would be available in a few days. I asked a few questions and thanked him. A tremendous sense of relief swept over me.

I told Sue she could leave, but she wanted to stay until we could see my husband. That required two more hours of waiting. I shared with her some ideas about an article I was writing, and we felt lighthearted and in good humor. We saw Dick, ate lunch together, and Sue left about 2:00 P.M.

Some time later I perceived the parallel between Sue's watching and waiting with me through my hours of fear and the disciples' watching and waiting in Gethsemane with Jesus. Sue did a much better job than the disciples! They fell asleep. I wish Jesus could have called upon Sue instead of Peter, James, and John.

I reflected on how I might have felt had Sue fallen asleep. What if she had arrived and said, "I've been really busy lately. Let's find a quiet spot so I can catch a nap."? Then I would have sat alone but worse than alone, because the one whose presence I counted on was not there. Not once but twice the disciples fell asleep. How this trivialized the agony of Jesus! The agitation and grief facing Jesus in his impending death far exceeded any anxiety about my husband's surgery, so the disciples' slight is magnified!

Watching and waiting brings some requirements: a prior close relationship, attentive presence, openness and listening, time, patience. Watching and waiting does not require a brilliant mind, professional expertise, or strong opinions. Watching and waiting is a form of ministry needed at many junctures in life. People wait for opportunities for more education or a job change, for a child to mature, for an appreciation of their abilities, for resolution of conflict. Perhaps the failure of the disciples and Jesus' subsequent forgiveness can encourage all of us to be there for others in their hours of need.

For Group Discussion or Personal Reflection

1. Tell about an occasion when someone waited with you through a time of anxiety and stress.

2. Compare the author's story with an experience of surgery you or a loved one has had. What was similar? Different?

3. Focus on the current illness of your loved one. Tell about people who waited with you through surgery, diagnosis, or treatment.

4. If you went through watching and waiting alone, how did it feel?

5. Read the Gethsemane text: Matthew 26:36–38, 40.

> Why was Jesus anxious and stressed?
> Whom did he choose to wait and watch with him?
> How did they fail him?
> How do you think Jesus felt?
> How does this story make you feel?
> What can you learn from this story?

6. What has an illness taught you about watching and waiting?

7. What is required of someone to be a good support for another in times of anxiety? Think of qualities of the person who waited with you (question number 1).

8. What are some ways you might be more supportive of others who are watching and waiting?

Be to me a rock of refuge, a strong fortress, to save me, ❖ ❖ ❖ for you are my rock and fortress. ❖ ❖ ❖

Psalm 71:3

3

Images of Strength

THE BOOK OF PSALMS is a prayer book used by people of faith, Jews and Christians, through many centuries. Whenever brokenness enters our lives, we look for resources to guide and sustain us through the time of pain. During the process of diagnosis and treatment of my husband's cancer, I continued my practice of reading the daily lectionary Bible texts. Most of the psalms used in this book simply came up in my daily readings. I was amazed that the psalms became such a great source of strength and hope to me.

The psalms cover a wide range of subjects, both joyful and sorrowful. The writers appear to experience and reflect on the total scope of life. It's a book for people living in the extremes. Some of the psalms are dark, angry, accusatory. Others reflect hope, optimism, trust. The writers are able to articulate deep feelings that perhaps we cannot. In the process of praying the psalms, we recognize our own soul's cry and surface and affirm that cry as part of our being.

Certain images of God from psalms became particularly helpful to me during these dark times. The prayer in Psalm 71 is addressed to God. See how the writer pictures God:

> Be to me a rock of refuge,
> a strong fortress, to save me,
> for you are my rock and my fortress.
>
> —*Psalm 71:3*

Note images of a strong God: rock, refuge, fortress. These are not words for normal times. In ordinary periods we may prefer to picture God as loving, kind, tenderhearted. But this text uses war words. They call us to battle. A rock becomes a firm foundation upon which to stand. A fortress surrounds and protects us when we are assaulted by the enemy. A refuge hides us when evil is pursuing. When we or loved ones are seriously ill, we feel weak, vulnerable, confused. Images of strength are just what we need in fearful times.

During an illness, some people come forth with support. Probably one supportive person is a doctor or someone else in the medical community. When struck with a disease, we may have little knowledge about it. We have no idea what to expect in the future or even if we can anticipate a future. We feel incredibly "needy." We meet someone who can describe the illness, put some fears to rest, and presumably facilitate a cure. Strong feelings of dependence toward medical personnel who provide this kind of support are natural, though the medical professionals may wish the feelings were not so strong. But in order to move forward, we must trust someone, and they are the ones there for us.

In the process of illness, we may also discover family members, friends, coworkers, church members, pastors, and others who emerge as sources of strength. Sometimes these are people whom we least expect. But in their own way, they provide support with a telephone call, a loaf of home-baked bread, an original poem at just the right time, a special card.

Under ordinary circumstances we trust ourselves to think and act. Illness can knock out all the props. False securities collapse. Then we have no option but to trust others and God. At such times, ancient images of strength can help sustain us. Martin Luther's stirring hymn "A Mighty Fortress Is Our God" is rich with such images.

A Mighty Fortress Is Our God

A mighty fortress is our God, a bulwark never failing;
our helper he amid the flood of mortal ills prevailing.
For still our ancient foe doth seek to work us woe;
his craft and power are great, and armed with cruel hate,
on earth is not his equal.

Did we in our own strength confide, our striving would
    be losing;
were not the right man on our side, the Man of God's
    own choosing.
Dost ask who that may be? Christ Jesus, it is he,
Lord Sabaoth, his name, from age to age the same,
and he must win the battle.

And though this world, with devils filled, should threaten
    to undo us,
we will not fear, for God hath willed his truth to
    triumph through us.
The Prince of Darkness grim, we tremble not for him;
his rage we can endure, for lo, his doom is sure;
one little word shall fell him.

That word above all earthly powers, no thanks to
    them, abideth;
the Spirit and the gifts are ours, thru him who with us sideth.
Let goods and kindred go, this mortal life also;
the body they may kill; God's truth abideth still;
his kingdom is forever.

—Martin Luther, ca. 1529

For Group Discussion or Personal Reflection

1. The author says serious illness can "knock out all our props." Has this happened to you during the illness of your loved one? If so, describe how it feels.

2. Tell about a person you know or have read about whom you see as a "tower of strength." What are some qualities of this person? How do you think he or she developed these qualities?

3. Identify persons or groups who have given you strength during your loved one's illness. What actions did they take that helped you?

4. Tell about literature that has sustained you through this illness. Why was it helpful? Does your list include the Bible?

5. Study the hymn "A Mighty Fortress Is our God." Which stanza is most helpful to you now? Explain. Memorize that stanza and sing or repeat it as needed in the days ahead.

6. Are the pictures of God from Psalm 71:3 helpful? Why or why not? What images of God do you have during good times? During bad times? Explain.

   Option: Using art supplies, draw or diagram an image of God that is meaningful to you at this time.

On my bed when I think of you,
 I muse on you
        in the watches of the night,
for you have always been my help;
 in the shadow of your wings
        I rejoice;

  my heart clings to you
 your right hand supports me.

Psalm 63:6-8, NJB

4

Praying through Stress

Y HUSBAND DID NOT SLEEP with me in the early nights of his illness. He experienced intense night sweats and fever. His body desperately tried to fight off the cancer situated in his abdominal area. The most stressful time was a period of about four weeks when we knew a lymphoma was present but did not know the precise diagnosis of Hodgkin's disease. The inability to name the enemy immobilized us.

The middle of the night always felt the worst. I would wake up with a heavy, gray feeling. My imagination would race, conjuring up fearful pictures. I dreaded the worst and could find no hope anywhere in the still darkness. Worry overwhelmed me!

After a period, I would try to pull my fragmented thoughts together and recall my breath prayer. I started by counting deliberately with each breath, from one to ten. Inhale and exhale, one; inhale and exhale, two . . . until peace and calm began to return. Then with each breath I would pray my breath prayer, "You are my God, I trust in you," over and over again. Sometimes I could remain in control, but sometimes scary thoughts crowded in again.

Breath prayer is an ancient prayer form experiencing a revival today. I chose this particular breath prayer at a retreat a few years ago. There we spent time meditating alone on an Old Testament psalm. This phrase from the psalm seemed meaningful to me then and has served me since. It implies a total letting go and letting God take charge. If at any time my needs change, I can choose another prayer.

The foundational biblical concept of breath prayer is a belief that our breath comes as a gift from God. "The spirit of God has made me, and the breath of the Almighty gives me life" (Job 33:4). In Hebrew the word for "breath" and the word for "spirit" are the same. The spirit that creates the earth (Genesis 1:2) is the same breath that animates all creatures (Psalm 104:30); both come from God. Without breath there is no life, and without life, no breath. When God breathes into humans the breath of life in Genesis 2:7, the writer of that account is expressing the profound truth that God is the source of our being. Life can be gifted to the next generation, but only God can create life. All life is really God's life. "In God we live and move and have our being" (Acts 17:28). The breath prayer enables us to draw upon the life of God and also connect with God's other creatures. The flow of air among us provides physical evidence of that connection.

To create your own breath prayer, identify what you need from God. Write down some general ideas. Look to scripture for expressions of your need and God's answer to your need or simply state the need. Shape your thoughts into a phrase of six to eight syllables, to fit with one inhalation and exhalation. You might choose words from a psalm or favorite hymn. Here are some examples:

- ♪ Hold me Lord, in your loving arms.
- ♪ You are my God, I trust in you.
- ♪ Thank you God, for giving me life.
- ♪ O Lord my God, you are very great (Psalm 104:1).
- ♪ The Lord is my shepherd, I shall not want (Psalm 23:1).
- ♪ The Lord is my light and salvation (Psalm 27:1).
- ♪ Have pity on me Lord, for I am weak (Psalm 6:3).
- ♪ Heal me Lord, for my bones are trembling (Psalm 6:3).

The ancient Jesus prayer fits best with two breaths:

Lord Jesus Christ, Son of God, have mercy on me, a sinner.

Many people of faith have regular disciplined times of prayer each day. In times of serious illness, however, the one stricken may be in pain, and you may be too busy providing care to pray in usual ways.

In both cases those involved may be too stressed to think. At such times, a breath prayer can soothe and reconnect us with the spirit of other creatures and with God.

You might encourage your loved one to create a breath prayer. You and others might wish to use that prayer at times particularly stressful for the patient. When it is difficult for the patient to pray personally, it is comforting to know that others are interceding on one's behalf.

For Group Discussion or Personal Reflection

1. Describe a former time of stress in your life. Who or what helped you through it?

2. What has been or is the most difficult situation connected with the current illness of your loved one? Who or what helped (or is helping) you through it?

3. During stressful periods, have you been able to pray? How do your prayers during stress differ from prayers during more peaceful times? What might you learn from this difference?

4. What new ideas did you get from the biblical background about God's breath as the source of all life? How might the information be helpful in dealing with this current illness?

5. Using the suggestions in this chapter, create your own breath prayer. Close your eyes and in silence count from one to ten as you inhale and exhale. Then add your own personal prayer words. Simply tell God what you need. How might you use the prayer later?

6. If your sick loved one believes in prayer, encourage him or her to create a breath prayer. Discuss how others might use it to intercede on his or her behalf.

7. Do you believe prayer can bring peace to you and your loved one during this present illness? Why or why not?

We are well aware that God works with those who love him, those who have been called in accordance with his purpose, and turns everything to their ✤ good. ✤

Romans 8:28, NJB

5

Journaling through Illness

MY HUSBAND RECEIVED his diagnosis of lymphoma the week before Mother's Day. As a Mother's Day gift my son and daughter-in-law sent a flowered notebook with a photo of me and my two grandsons inserted on the cover. I decided the notebook would serve as my personal journal through my husband's illness. Here I could record my fears, my joys, my search for God, as Dick and I walked through this difficult time. It was something I would do for myself.

I had kept a daily journal off and on at other periods in my life. At the advent of Dick's illness, I was not doing so. I realized, however, that during this time of radical disorientation, I needed to write in order to maintain a sense of order. Helen Keller, deaf and blind since early childhood, recounted that before she learned words, her life seemed chaotic. Once her teacher began tracing words onto her hand and she associated words with objects, her world took on order. Words order our experiences.

Words also help identify emotions. By naming a feeling, we begin to tame it. Our anger, jealousy, impatience, are no longer floating freely and causing damage. An emotion does not boomerang, hurting those close as well as ourselves. When we name our feelings, they become more manageable. Remember the saying: "Name it, claim it, tame it."

In a traumatic situation, such as life-threatening illness, so much happens so fast that we cannot possibly handle emotions as events occur. We feel as if we are on a runaway train. We find it difficult to cope. If we journal, we can return repeatedly to the scene and reprocess events. We relive the sensations and grow comfortable with them. Gradually we begin to find some resolution. A journal is like a bin with many feelings, events, and people thrown in as brief references. Later, we go back into our bin and pull out these raw ideas for refinement through further writing, reflection, and action.

Another benefit of journaling is the revelation of what some regard as "touchstones," pockets of joy in the midst of our confusion. We can go back to these and relive the happy moments. On a conscious level I recall my husband's illness as a heavy time. When I reread my journal, however, I am struck with the good times sandwiched in among the bad. I recorded summer days lit with brilliant sunlight when we sat together on the deck, our pastor's prayer in our living room, a friend calling the evening before surgery with good wishes. I wrote about wonderful qualities of patience and strength in my husband, which I had not noticed before. If these touchstones had not been recorded, I might have remained mired in distress, but now these precious times are available to me always, whenever I need refreshment.

Journaling challenges us to notice and record deeper feelings about God. Where is God in all this? we ask ourselves. We write one observation one day, something different on another occasion. Each seems an isolated manifestation of God's love in the midst of the illness. But because we have noted and recorded, we can return to our journal later and discern patterns of God's spirit acting in the dramatic events, the people, and the healing process. We see a rhythm of goodness dancing through our experiences. When we begin to notice God, our faith increases, we watch and listen more intently, and we develop "eyes to see and ears to hear"—further movements of the Spirit.

How does one begin journaling? Get yourself a notebook, mark it "Private," and lock it or hide it away. Fear of someone's reading your thoughts may prove inhibiting. Try to write every day, but if you miss, it's OK. Put the date and place of writing on each entry. Write freely and easily in any form you wish. Don't worry about grammar, punctuation, and the like or you'll get bogged down. Do not bring judgment to your experiences. Write what you honestly feel—not what you think you should feel. If you don't like to express yourself in writing, try pictures, diagrams, whatever works.

The most common form of journaling is the daily log. This is the bin into which we throw things as they happen, often in short, fragmented style. We might then go back later, pull out ideas and process them through further writing. We can enlarge on the scene, replay the sensations, and gain clarity.

Dreams are also good fodder for our bins. We can record and hold them for subsequent reflection and interpretations. Ambivalent feelings may be examined through imaginary dialogues or monologues addressed to a person—for example, your doctor, pastor, parent. You might wish to carry on an imaginary dialogue with a spiritual person from your past, even one who is dead. You could choose a person in scriptures. Ask for advice. Listen and record his or her words of wisdom to you.

You might write a dialogue with your loved one's illness or with a part of your own body that is experiencing pain or stress. If this illness has required that you relinquish your job, address your former work, telling how it was fulfilling or not and how you feel about giving it up. While these situations may appear contrived, people are often surprised by repressed feelings that emerge when imagination is given free reign.

Some people find scripture and prayer prepare them for a deeper level of writing. Some prefer background music, while others like silence. Some may use taped guided meditations, relaxation exercises, or focus on breathing to get in touch with the spirit within. Whatever works for you is fine!

If journaling proves helpful to you, recommend it to your loved one who is ill. He or she may gain strength from the process also.

By journaling, we bring order to the deeper levels of our lives. When we observe that order, we grow confident that a holy pattern exists, working to bring good out of evil, even in the midst of our anxiety and pain.

For Group Discussion or Personal Reflection

1. Do you like to read? If so, what kind of books? Identify a favorite book and talk or think about why you enjoy it.

2. Do you like to write? If so, what type of writing (letters, reports, stories, poetry, other)? What do you like about that kind of writing? If you do not like to write, what are some ways in which you like to express yourself?

3. If you have journaled at any time, tell about the experience. Was it helpful or not? Why do you think this was so?

4. What has been one of the most difficult situations connected with the illness of your loved one? Who or what helped you through? Did you try journaling? Was that process helpful? If you did not keep a journal, consider whether doing so might have been helpful. Explain.

5. Describe at least one "touchstone" during this current illness, that is, a pocket of joy in the midst of chaos.

6. Do you believe that God works to turn things to good for those who love God (Romans 8:28)? How does this belief affect the way you view this present illness?

While they were eating, Jesus took a loaf of bread, and after blessing it he broke it, gave it to the disciples, and said,

" TAKE, EAT;
THIS IS MY BODY."

Then he took a cup, and after giving thanks he gave it to them saying,

" DRINK FROM IT,
ALL OF YOU;
FOR THIS IS MY BLOOD
OF THE COVENANT,
WHICH IS POURED OUT
FOR MANY
FOR THE FORGIVENESS OF SINS."

MATTHEW 26:26~28

6

Blood as the Source of Life

HILE MY HUSBAND was so sick, I attended our church alone. He could not gather energy to do much of anything. On one of those Sundays we received the sacrament of the Lord's Supper. When I heard the reading of Jesus' invitation, "This is my blood. Drink from it, all of you," I recalled the biblical understanding of blood as the source of life. I was weary of illness and I needed an infusion of energy. I claimed the symbol of Jesus' shedding blood so many years ago as a means of renewing my energy that day.

Ancient religions focused upon sacrifice. In primitive times a virtuous human was chosen for the honor of serving as a sacrifice. Later, an unblemished lamb was substituted. (For the basis of the Jewish Passover tradition, see Exodus 12:21-27.) In the Christian tradition, the blood of Jesus, the lamb of God, was shed for all and became the final sacrifice necessary for empowerment and new life (see 1 Peter 1:18-19).

All these religious traditions assumed blood to be the source of life. They held that the flow of blood from a sacrificed victim released creative energy. Life literally spilled out onto the altar. The victim died, but participants in the ritual were revitalized from its shed blood. The sacrificed life released power which flowed freely among all. New life was never possible without death. Life continually moved through cycles of suffering and death and back to new life.

Thus blood symbolizes new life, but it does much more. A symbol is not just a sign, something pointing to another reality. It is more

45

than a picture meant to recall a truth. Rather the symbol itself contains an element of coincidence. The symbol of blood does not just point toward or remind us of energy, but energy actually exists in blood. I am awed to realize that ancient people's sense of blood as the source of energy preceded verification by modern science.

My husband's first symptom of illness was fatigue. Blood tests were central to the diagnostic process. We were introduced to a world of neutrophils, lymphocytes, monocytes, hemoglobin, hematocrit, platelets. Blood was drawn, redrawn, compared. As the numbers plunged, so did Dick's energy.

When Dick was extremely tired, I would lie on the bed beside him and place my hand upon his arm. "I am going to give some of my energy to you," I would say. "Can you feel energy flowing through my blood into you?" "Yes, I can feel it," he would respond. I discovered that in frightening situations, we rely upon intuition rather than intellect, and this was one such time.

When my husband finally received his first chemotherapy treatment for Hodgkin's disease, his hemoglobin count was at seven and he could barely walk from the hospital parking lot to the treatment area. The next day he received a blood transfusion. I felt grateful to whoever had shared the gift of life. I told Dick he deserved it, because he had given blood many times at Red Cross blood drives. Now it was his turn to receive the precious gift. An increase in energy seemed noticeable even before we left the hospital.

The sacrament of Holy Communion (Eucharist), when understood as a release of life-giving blood, can be a source of power and energy to those burdened by the weariness of illness. The symbol of blood can remain imprinted within our memory and continue to refresh us through subsequent days. The symbol contains power to metabolize pain into energy.

"This is my blood. Drink from it, all of you."

For Group Discussion or Personal Reflection

1. The cycle of death and new life can occur many times within our lifetime. Examples might be new insights, changed relationships, accepting or giving forgiveness, moving to another location, gaining control of an addiction, relinquishing a fear. Tell about a time in your own experience when you moved through death to new life.

   Option: Using art supplies, create a symbol of your transformation from death to new life. Share with one other person in the group.

2. The scripture texts show that Jesus used the symbol of blood, also a symbol of the Passover and the Israelites' passage from slavery (death) to freedom (life), to give meaning to his own death and resurrection. Did you gain new insights about Holy Communion (Eucharist) from this section? Talk about your understanding of this sacrament.

3. Has the condition of your loved one's blood been an important consideration during the process of diagnosis and treatment of cancer? Explain. Does the ancient understanding of blood as a source of energy and life provide any new perspective on that experience?

4. Who and what have become sources of energy for you as caregiver during this current illness? What are some new sources of energy that might be available to you now? How might you tap into these?

Jesus said . . .
"Come to me, all you that are weary
and are carrying heavy burdens,
and I will give you rest."

Matthew 11:25, 28

Be still,
and know
that I am
God!

Psalm 46:10

7

Sick Time as Holy Time

UNE WAS OUR worst month, the time Dick was experiencing pain and was unable to eat due to the pressure of enlarged abdominal lymph nodes on other organs. His fatigue was overwhelming and night sweats continued. That period also brought the stress of waiting for diagnostic surgery. Yet I wrote the following as part of my journal entries:

June 2—The weather remains sunshiny and brilliant and all will turn out OK. These days bring their own beauty. Life is much slower. Our energies focus on one thing—healing. Dick and I are more intimate. We receive much love and concern from so many people. Our days are lived on a deeper level, closer to emotions and to the Spirit.

June 17—These summer days are incredibly lovely. I took it easy yesterday, sat in the sun, finished my novel. Dick's illness has slowed us down and it is very nice!

Before he became ill, my husband had been planning to go to part-time retirement. His replacement was hired in February, and in April Dick went to a part-time schedule. In spite of his low energy, he went to work every day. His interest in his work remained high, and he would never have missed an important meeting. In early May, we got the diagnosis of lymphoma. By mid-May, his fatigue was so debilitating he simply could not work any longer.

Six months later, Dick was stopping in at work occasionally, planning full retirement, and enjoying the good life. Illness had slowed him down, caused him to reevaluate priorities and to develop other interests. It occurred to me during these more leisurely months that sick time is holy time.

Throughout history, people of faith divided time into two segments: ordinary time and holy time. Ordinary time is a period between sacred events, such as religious holidays, plus the six days between Sabbaths. Holy time is quality time set apart from ordinary time. During holy time religious people live in deeper communion with creation and the Creator.

By means of liturgy, rituals, and stories, people pass from ordinary to sacred time and back again into the secular world. For example, the call to worship in most weekly Sunday services invites people from the secular to the sacred. The benediction (closing blessing) returns them to the world to serve.

In a similar way, when we are open to God's movements, diagnosis of an illness may be experienced as the "call" introducing us to holy time, while restoration to health returns us to the world. If the illness results in death, the person remains in holy time. Heaven is sometimes understood as the eternal Sabbath.

In the biblical creation story, God completed work on the sixth day, and on the seventh, God ceased from work. He blessed the seventh day and made it holy (Genesis 2:1-3). Sabbath brings refreshment to the whole creation, as all creatures stop and enjoy the mystery and beauty of the good world made by God (Exodus 20:8-11). Sabbath is different from other religious holidays, because God, the Holy One, named it holy. (For most Christians, Sunday is the day of worship because the first day of the week recalls the resurrection of Jesus.)

Holy means blessed, set apart as special. Scholars tell us the root Hebrew word for *holy* is the same as that for *healing*. Thus, holy time heals us from the frenzied, stressful activity of ordinary time and provides a rhythm of work and rest, engagement and retreat. Sick time is "enforced leisure" and brings a chance for reveling in an extended period of holy time.

The dualism of ordinary and holy time might be described with the following contrasts:

ORDINARY TIME	HOLY TIME
work	*rest*
achievement	*reflection*
effort	*relaxation*
noise	*solitude*
cultivating earth	*enjoying earth*
acquiring money	*sharing material goods*
seeking answers	*accepting mystery*
stress	*peace*
outward	*inward*
doing	*being*

The advent of illness is like walking into a darkened room. At first it's scary, and we cannot see anything clearly. As our eyes adjust, however, the darkness seems more familiar. We can see better now. But we see quite differently than we do in the sunlight. Reality is suffused with a soft misty quality. We become comfortable with the unique beauty of the dark. We begin to trust the emptiness and silence. Our fear turns to gratitude as we perceive in the darkness what we never saw in the light. We live in holy time and holy space.

"Be still and know that I am God" (Psalm 46:10).

For Group Discussion or Personal Reflection

1. As the illness of your loved one has progressed—
    a) How has it affected your relationship to your own work?
    b) Has this change been welcome or upsetting?
    c) How have you resolved tensions between the demands of your present responsibilities and the patient's needs?

2. Have you experienced this illness as holy time, as described by the writer? Explain. In what ways has your experience been similar? Different?

3. During your time as caregiver, have any particular aspects of God's creation become special to you, such as,
    a) a location in nature (a park, garden, or walking place)?
    b) creatures (pets, birds, wild animals)?
    c) plants (flowers or plants in your room, a forest, a single tree)?
    d) natural phenomena (sunrises or sunsets, storms, snowfall)?
    e) appetizing foods?

4. Does an element of nature special to you contribute to your own emotional and spiritual health during this illness? Explain.

5. The writer contrasts characteristics of ordinary time and holy time. Cross off any pairs in the list on page 51 that you think should not be listed. Add others. Does your holy-time list match your perception of sick time?

6. Is the metaphor of entering a darkened room a suitable one to describe this present illness for you? If not, how would you describe the experience? What do you "see more clearly" as you sojourn with your loved one in sick time?

7. During this illness, do you feel God's presence more than in ordinary time? In what ways? Why do you think this is so? If not, how might you be more open to God's presence?

Be gracious to me,

O God,

be gracious;
for I have made thee
my refuge.

I will take refuge
in the shadow of thy

until the storms
are past.

Psalm 57:1, NEB

8

Setting Up Boundaries

WE ALL NEED BOUNDARIES around our own inner self, a safe place where others may not intrude. We balance between extroversion and introversion, engagement and retreat. During a serious illness, it is necessary to be clear about our own boundaries and those of loved ones. It's natural to feel anger when safe areas are violated and essential to defend them.

One of the low spots for us during my husband's illness came when our oncologist explained chemotherapy and possible side effects. During that session the doctor said Dick needed to receive a succession of three injections to counter the effects of chemotherapy treatment. The shots would boost his white blood count and prevent his succumbing to infection. Our doctor looked at me and suggested I might learn to give the shots to avoid returning to the hospital on three successive days after treatments. I could feel myself shrinking into the back of my chair.

The next Monday when we arrived for Dick's first chemo treatment, the nurse asked if I wanted to learn to give my husband the shots and I replied affirmatively. It seemed the least I could do when he was going through such difficult treatment. I watched the nurse give the injection and then took home a video with complete instructions.

On Tuesday we traveled to the hospital for Dick's blood transfusion. We had experienced a horrendous night after his first chemo. Dick was extremely fatigued and I was stressed. The nurse said if I could give the shot at the hospital under supervision the following day, we could do it at home on Friday. I felt uncomfortable with a timetable. The nurse graciously took me through the process and then said, "OK, what is step one?" I could not remember.

I lay awake and worried during the night. Finally, I decided the most I could do for the moment was survive the illness, and it was all I needed to do. When we arrived at the hospital Wednesday morning, I told the nurse firmly that I had decided not to give the injection. I never again watched it administered, never wavered in my resolve. I knew what I could handle and became comfortable with my boundaries. I did find two willing persons in our town to give my husband shots, and eventually Dick gave them to himself.

In addition to setting up boundaries about what we can do, Dick and I discovered that illness requires limits on how much information we wish to receive. Some assume it best to know everything about a diagnosis. I now believe this is not always true. The choice belongs to the patient and loved ones. In a life-threatening situation, we can take only one step at a time, and keeping up confidence and hope becomes paramount.

According to literature from the hospital, our doctor would take his cue from us regarding how much to tell us. We realized early on if we wanted to know, we needed to ask.

In our first session after diagnosis, we asked our doctor some questions, and he answered them directly and honestly. He did not violate our boundaries; we invited him to step across but then experienced regret. The doctor went on to share more information than we could handle at that point. Dick and I felt both alarmed and dispirited. My husband told me he wanted to set that bit of information aside for now. He needed a safe environment in which to begin healing. He set up a temporary boundary, and I respected it. We did not talk of the matter for a number of months, because we would have gained nothing by doing so.

A friend's husband has cancer. After a particularly harrowing surgery and subsequent infection, a hospital doctor (not their personal physician) informed her that her husband probably had only about a year to live. She had not asked. The doctor imposed information on her which she did not want. She reacted angrily. When the doctor said her husband needed to know, she physically blocked him from the room. My friend felt the doctor had violated her boundaries and assaulted her hope. I believe she had every right to her anger.

In addition to boundaries around what we can do and limits on information we wish to receive, both patient and caregiver deserve places of refuge. During the most stressful times of my husband's illness, I fenced out reality by reading novels. I chose to read books by favorite authors that perked up my spirits. For a few hours in the evening I sat on my back porch and smiled about romantic escapades in England in the early 1800s. I retreated into another world and found relief. I never felt guilty for setting up space for retreat.

Your home can become an important refuge. If pain or stress is intense and privacy desired, say no to well-meaning visitors. Tell them you will invite them back later when the situation is improved.

During difficult times our personal boundaries may fluctuate more than usual. We may desire solitude one day and hugs the next. We need to stay tuned to our own emotions and act accordingly.

For Group Discussion or Personal Reflection

1. Tell a story about a time during your loved one's illness when your privacy was violated. How did you feel? Did you take any action?

2. Tell a story about a time during this illness when someone entered your private space and you welcomed the action. Why do you think it was helpful in that situation? What might it teach us about crossing boundaries?

3. In this exercise, you'll make two drawings to illustrate your own private space during this illness.
    a) *How my private space is occupied now:* Draw a fenced square and place yourself in the middle. Place people and objects you feel

are in your space now inside the fence and those that are distant on the outside.

b) *How I wish it were*: Draw a fenced square and place yourself in the middle. Place people and objects you wish were close to you inside the fence and those you wish were not close to you on the outside.

Explain your pictures to one other person. What might you do to make the second picture a reality?

4. What are some ways you retreat for renewal during times of stress? Have you allowed adequate time for renewal during this illness? If not, how might you begin to do so?

5. Reread Psalm 57:1. Have you experienced God as a refuge during stormy times? Explain. If not, what is one thing you might do to allow this to happen?

all who hate me
whisper together about me;
they imagine the worst for me;
they think that a deadly thing
has fastened on me,
that i will not rise again
from where i lie.
even my bosom friend
in whom i trusted,
who ate of my bread,
has lifted the heel
against me.

psalm 41:7-9

9

Tearing Down Boundaries

EELINGS OF abandonment, real or imagined, may come with the onset of cancer. Disease includes a social dimension. Patterns of relationships change. Old boundaries fluctuate. Needs may increase and responses diminish. The sick person must deal not only with physical deterioration but with inner emotional turmoil as well. Physical illness never arrives alone. It carries emotional, social, and spiritual baggage.

Sometimes it is the patient who contributes to social separation. He or she may feel uncomfortable talking about the disease. There may be scars, disfiguring surgeries, artificial devices, hair loss, and other changes in appearance which cause embarrassment. Sometimes anger, despair, and physical pain motivate the ill person to retreat from relationships. The caregiver may be caught between the desire to protect the loved one and the need for outside support.

On the other side, it may be friends and family who withdraw. Some may handle the diagnosis well, but others may find themselves unable to continue as usual. Fear of saying the wrong thing, witnessing pain, or facing the death of a loved one, can all prove inhibiting. Some people may be poorly informed and actually think cancer is contagious. Perhaps those who set up boundaries truly care, but their fears work to alter a previously positive relationship.

Some boundaries may get erected during a serious illness, but more often, I believe, boundaries do come down. My husband received chemotherapy every other week for six months. Following that, he received radiation treatments at a different hospital but periodically returned to the first cancer treatment center to get his medi-port flushed. One Friday I sat in the waiting room while he had the procedure done. As I read my magazine, I overheard a conversation between two distraught women. Under other circumstances I would not have intruded into a discussion between strangers. But this time I reached across boundaries.

"What kind of cancer does your son have?" I inquired of one woman, obviously the mother.

"He was just diagnosed with a lymphoma," she replied. "He is so sick. We took him to the emergency room a number of times with severe pains, but they missed all the symptoms. He experiences night sweats and so far has lost about thirty pounds."

"My husband has a lymphoma too—Hodgkin's disease," I said. "He was diagnosed six months ago and is progressing well. As soon as he started chemo treatment his pain left, he resumed eating, and his night sweats disappeared."

We talked and I tried to reassure them. I recognized in the mother the surface tears, the desperate glances, the signs of panic I had experienced during the period of Dick's diagnosis. Dick came back to the waiting room, looking happy and strong. The woman asked whether he would go and talk with her son. Dick went with the mother to the treatment area and tried to speak words of encouragement.

When they returned, the mother thanked us and said to Dick, "You are the only other person I ever met who has lymphoma." We exchanged phone numbers and wished one another well.

Common suffering creates immediate bonds. Pain is shareable. It compels us to empathize with others in similar situations. Accepting pain is a schooling in compassion. When one has suffered, one cannot forget the feeling nor fail to recognize it in others. I needed to reach out to that woman. I wanted to diminish her anxiety by telling about my own. We shared a common link that transcended ordinary boundaries.

All through his illness, Dick and I both received strong support from family, coworkers, neighbors, and church members. But those most present for us were others who had survived cancer. A woman in our town, whom I did not know well, wrote me a beautiful note. Her husband had lung cancer. I responded and then she came over with information on lymphoma from the Internet, tapes, videos, and much encouragement. She proved a valuable friend through the ordeal.

Many people in our church responded, but especially helpful were those who had survived cancer. The mention of my husband's name in prayers of the congregation every Sunday gave us inspiration and hope. Our own pastor survived Hodgkin's disease twenty years ago and is now hale and hearty. His ministry to us during this time proved a great blessing. Issues that previously divided now seemed trivial, and supportive love was all that mattered.

Dick's chemotherapy treatments lasted a number of hours, so while waiting for him I attended the cancer support group that met at the center every Tuesday. People previously unknown to each other gathered and shared their pain, fears, and hopes. Some came in wheelchairs, some cried, some asked for prayers. Some felt nauseated from chemotherapy, some suffered physical discomfort, some faced serious surgeries. Yet others told of medications that eased pain, treatments that helped, remissions of many years, and cures. Many continued to come to the meetings long after their cure, just to encourage others. The meetings were never depressing. I always left feeling uplifted. The reason, of course, is that sharing pain and fears diminishes them.

One young woman in the support group, Carol, had a cancer metastasized to a number of areas of her body. She looked incredibly fragile and faced a stem-cell transplant. Every time it was mentioned she said, "I am so afraid." Yet there at the meeting was Mary, who had received a stem-cell transplant a number of years earlier, looking bright, cheerful, and healthy. She encouraged Carol, called her on the phone, and reported back on Carol's progress in the weeks after the procedure when she was confined to the hospital. Sharing pain energizes for the journey through darkness.

My husband sometimes serves as worship leader in our church. A period of about six months elapsed before he felt well enough to return to the pulpit. On his first Sunday back, he welcomed people to worship, thanked them for their prayers during his illness, and said it was wonderful to be back leading worship again. Applause broke out as everyone in the congregation expressed joy at his progress. Shared joy, as well as shared pain, tears down boundaries.

> I have told the glad news of deliverance
> in the great congregation;
> see I have not restrained my lips,
>   as you know, O Lord.
> I have not hidden your saving help within my heart,
> I have spoken of your faithfulness and your salvation;
> I have not concealed your steadfast love and your
>   faithfulness
> from the great congregation.
>
> —*Psalm 40:9-10*

For Group Discussion or Personal Reflection

1. Tell about a time during the illness of your loved one when some-one reached across a boundary to help you. How did you respond? Why?

2. Tell about a situation during this illness when you felt abandoned by someone from whom you expected support. Why do you think this happened? How did it make you feel? Did you do anything to try to remedy the situation? Why or why not?

3. Do you participate in a support group for people with cancer and their families? If so, is it helpful? Explain.

4. If you are a member of an organized religious community, what roles do people from this group play during this present illness and treatment? Have their responses been encouraging or disappointing? Describe some specific instances.

5. Reread Psalm 40:9-10 at the end of this chapter. Have you found an opportunity to "tell the glad news of God's deliverance in the great congregation"? Explain. How might your religious community better facilitate such sharing?

Praise for Healing through Restoration to Health
~ Psalm 116

A Reading
for use in family, support group, or other communal setting

Leader: I love the Lord, because he has heard my voice and my supplications.

    All: Because he inclined his ear to me, therefore I will call on him as long as I live.

Leader: The snares of death encompassed me; the pangs of Sheol laid hold on me; I suffered distress and anguish.

    All: Then I called on the name of the Lord: "O Lord, I pray, save my life!"

Leader: Gracious is the Lord, and righteous; our God is merciful.

    All: The Lord protects the simple; when I was brought low, he saved me.

Leader: Return, O my soul, to your rest, for the Lord has dealt bountifully with you.

    All: For you have delivered my soul from death, my eyes from tears, my feet from stumbling.

Leader: I walk before the Lord in the land of the living. . . .

All: What shall I return to the Lord for all his bounty to me?

Leader: I will lift up the cup of salvation and call on the name of the Lord, I will pay my vows to the Lord in the presence of all his people. . . .

All: O Lord, I am your servant; I am your servant, the child of your serving girl. You have loosed my bonds.

Leader: I will offer to you a thanksgiving sacrifice and call on the name of the Lord.

All: I will pay my vows to the Lord in the presence of all his people,

Leader: in the courts of the house of the Lord, in your midst, O Jerusalem.

All: Praise the Lord!

—Psalm 116: 1–9, 12–14, 16–19

Do not fear,
for I have redeemed you;
I have called you by name,

YOU
ARE
MINE.

When you pass
through the waters,
I will be with you;
and through the rivers,
they shall not overwhelm you...
For I am the Lord your God,
The Holy One of Israel,
your Savior.

Isaiah 43:1-2, 3

PART II

Walking through the Waters of Death

I said,
In the prime of life I must pass away;
for the rest of my days
I am consigned to the gates of Sheol.
I said, I shall no longer see the Lord
as I did in the land of the living;
I shall no longer see my fellow-men
as I did when I lived in the world.
My dwelling is taken from me,
pulled up like a shepherd's tent;
you have rolled up my life
like a weaver

when he cuts the web from the thrum.
Day and night you torment me.

Yet, Lord, because of you

My soul shall live?
Give my spirit rest;
restore me and give me life.

Isaiah 38:10-12, 16 REB

10

Dreams of Death

EVERYONE WHO faces a serious illness such as cancer or who has a family member facing such illness thinks about the possibility of death. Because it may be difficult to articulate feelings about death, we sometimes think in word pictures (images). King Hezekiah of Judah (eighth century B.C.E.) is no different. Writing after recovery from a serious illness, he draws two images of death in the text opposite.

In the first, he imagines his dwelling, that is, his body, as a tent, struck down and carried away from him. In the second, he pictures God as a weaver who folds up his life and cuts the last thread. Both of these images, the shepherd and the weaver, draw upon common life in that period.

Most of us avoid facing our own death or that of a loved one. Often we suppress these thoughts. While we are awake we may succeed in ignoring them, but in our sleep, when our consciousness is not on alert, these images push up into our minds in the form of dreams. Our mind forces us to confront them, but confusing images in dreams make it difficult to interpret the meaning. Dreams usually do not predict the future. They can, however, provide insight into our feelings and thus help facilitate our acceptance of them.

A number of weeks elapsed between the time my husband was told he had a lymphoma and the biopsy surgery required for a precise diagnosis. We did not talk of death because we wanted to keep up our spirits and remain optimistic. During that period, however, I experienced a very disturbing dream. I knew the images were important because the dream was accompanied by intense feelings, and I could not forget it.

I dreamed I was in a drab, dreary building, with walls painted a dark gray color. I ascended stairs to an upper floor and there found my husband in a room with a woman. The woman looked like a hag. She had blond hair in curlers, a cigarette in her mouth, sagging stockings, but she appeared seductive. My husband told me that he was leaving me for this woman. I was stunned and angry. If she had been beautiful and charming I might have understood, but his choosing such an ugly person over me hurt a lot.

The woman in the dream then sauntered down the stairs I had just ascended, and I rushed to the window to watch where she was going. She walked across the street into an institutional-looking building. She tossed her head and laughed cruelly as she called over her shoulder, "I live at Saginaw General Hospital." I knew immediately the ugly woman was my image of death, waiting to take my husband from me.

The fact that I could acknowledge the fears in my mind was helpful. When we suppress feelings, they don't really disappear. We cannot bypass them. They just gnaw away at the depth of our being. If we can surface an emotion, it may hurt, but we can talk or write or pray or cry over it. Once a feeling is named, it becomes more manageable and less frightening.

For Group Discussion or Personal Reflection

1. Tell about a disturbing dream you have had, either connected to this illness or at some other time. What did the dream reveal about your subconscious feelings?

2. King Hezekiah draws two images of death: (1) his body as a tent struck down and carried away and (2) God, like a weaver, folding up his life and cutting the last thread. Do either of these images carry meaning for you when thinking of your own death or that of your loved one? Why or why not?

3. These biblical images, the shepherd and the weaver, drew upon common life in that period. What picture of death might you draw from common life in our time? Is the picture comforting or disturbing for you?

   Option: Using art supplies draw an image of death from common life today.

4. In considering the possibility of the death of your loved one, what words best describe your current response: deny, ignore, suppress, confront, anger, panic, hurt, fear, prepare, accept.
   Other: _____

5. Have family members discussed the possibility of the death of your loved one? Choose a word or phrase to identify their response.

6. Have you talked about the possibility of his or her death with your sick loved one? What practical matters might need to be decided (finances, hospice care, funeral plans)? What emotional strength sought (counseling)? What spiritual care provided (prayer, anointing, reading of scriptures)?

For everything its season,
and for every activity under heaven
its time:
a time to be born and a time to die;
a time to plant and a time to uproot;
a time to kill and a time to heal;
a time to pull down and a time to build up;
a time to weep and a time to laugh;
a time for mourning and a time for dancing;
a time to scatter stones and
a time to gather them;
a time to embrace and
a time to refrain from embracing;
a time to seek and a time to lose;
a time to keep and a time to throw away;
a time to tear and a time to mend;
a time for silence and a time for speech;
a time to love and a time to hate;
a time for war and a time for peace.

Ecclesiastes 3:1-8, NEB

11

The Present Moment

WHAT TIME is it now? Is it a time to live or a time to die? a time to laugh or a time to cry? a time to cling or a time to let go? a time for mourning or a time for dancing? What season does this cancer bring? How can we discern the time?

The Old Testament writer of the poem from Ecclesiastes pairs opposites that represent the heights and depths of human life. Sick time is life in the heights and life in the depths. Events move forward rapidly; we feel out of control. Then love slows us down and we savor precious moments. Sometimes the highs and lows even coexist in the same moment.

My journal entry, July 7—Yesterday I felt good—today terrible. Dick passed a bad night with lots of pain. He took two pain pills and then slept. We were sure his lymph nodes had shrunk, but maybe they are coming back. Cancer is such a roller coaster!

During serious illness we confront life-and-death issues, and these bring an intensity of feelings not present in times of health. The author of Ecclesiastes writes, in the verses following the printed text, about what people gain from all their toil (3:10-14). He believes God makes everything to suit its time, gives humans a sense of past and future but no understanding of God's overall pattern. Therefore we should be happy and live the best life we can. We should eat and drink and enjoy ourselves because all is a gift from God. Because he believes God acts consistently forever, the biblical writer exhibits a sense of security within the insecurity of time. To this sense of security nothing can be added or taken away. The writer breaks free of a stressful life of worry and exhibits a remarkable freedom to embrace the present moment. He enjoys the ordinary pleasures of sweetness of sunlight (11:7), food, drink, and work (4:13), comfort and dressing up (9:8), youth (11:9), friendship (4:9-12), and the woman he loves (9:9). He finds joy in the present because he accepts it as God's gift.

Normally we travel life's path dragging fears from the past or projecting anxieties into the future. We rarely focus on the present. But during serious illness, the past becomes insignificant and the future is tenuous. The present dominates. Every moment matters as we move forward, one day at a time.

My journal entry, June 17—Tonight we are sitting together listening to beautiful classical music. Dick is half-asleep, but I know he is enjoying it. I am thinking this period is special because there is such intensity of feeling. Nothing is superficial. There exists deep anxiety and tension, even anger, and yet a recollection of wonderful times of love. Tears remain near the surface. A friend brought over homemade strawberry shortcake for supper tonight because, she said, she wanted to do something nice for us.

I was thinking how strong Dick is. He never complains about his loss of energy or the cramping pain. He continues to say everything will turn out all right. When I accuse the doctors of slowness, he tells me not to be negative. He encourages me to have confidence in them. I love him so much and I don't want to lose him yet.

The day we received the result of Dick's bone-marrow biopsy was far from an ordinary moment in time. The oncologist extracted the bone marrow on Monday, and we were to learn the results at 4:00 P.M. Wednesday. The doctor had told us, "Even if the cancer is in the bones, it does not necessarily result in the patient's demise." What a nice way to say Dick might die, I thought. I now know what he said is true, but in my fear, I decided if Dick's bones were clear he would live and if not, he probably would die.

On the day we were to receive test results, I went to a morning meeting because I decided it was better to stay busy. I remember every moment of that day: the clothes I wore, what I ate, people I saw. When I walked into the cancer center where the doctor's office was located, I passed a gift shop. I said to myself, *The next time I see that gift shop I will know whether he will live or die.* I met Dick in the waiting room, and as we were ushered down the hallway, our doctor was entering another room. He threw Dick a high sign, but I missed it. When we got into the room Dick said, "My bone marrow is clear." Great relief replaced our tensions. Perhaps after all, we would have more time.

Schedules for chemotherapy treatments, blood tests, injections, and more made it impossible to take an extended vacation. However, in mid-August we got the idea to take a short trip to Saugatuck, a quaint town across the state on the east shore of Lake Michigan. We left on Tuesday morning and returned Thursday evening. In the middle of a hot, dry summer, we got three damp, misty days. That made the setting even more cozy. We went to bed early and slept late. Our room at the bed-and-breakfast was decorated just right—all Victorian and peaceful. We walked on the beach in slickers, spotted a deer in the woods, lunched in an English pub with a fireplace ablaze. We ran between raindrops from one shop to the other, not buying much of anything, just having fun. We read, relaxed, talked with houseguests at breakfast, ate in unique restaurants. It was a wonderful reprieve!

My journal entry, September 15—After thirty-seven years of marriage, our love is deeper now than ever before. People give up so easily on love. It becomes much stronger after going through illness and hardship together. It's an anxious week because Dick had a CT scan yesterday and we get the report on Thursday.

The present moment, *now*, is what matters during serious illness. The highs and lows get all mixed in together. For me, the summer of '98 was, as the saying goes, the worst of times and the best of times:

My husband was diagnosed with cancer!

I fell in love all over again!

For Group Discussion or Personal Reflection

1. Reread Ecclesiastes 3:1–9. Think of the period of your loved one's illness as your present moment.
   a) What are some "timely" activities for you now?
   b) What activities might be "out of synch" with this situation?

2. Read the following section, Ecclesiastes 3:9–15.
   a) What part of human life do you believe will live on after your time on earth ends? (5:14–16)
   b) How might that belief affect the way you use your time now?
   c) Do you believe eating, drinking, and enjoying work is a gift from God? Explain.

3. What is the best thing that has happened to you during this present moment of illness? worst? If you can, give an example of the best and worst occurring to you at the same time.

4. Thinking of the present moment as your loved one's time of illness, write down answers to the following questions:
   a) When did this period begin? end?
   b) Describe your physical condition.
   c) Name the people important to you.
   d) Identify activities that engage you.
   e) What feelings dominate your life now?

5. Using answers listed in number 4, reflect quietly on your *now*, the present moment. When an idea comes, write about it. It might be a summary or refocusing statement, a hope, a prayer, an affirmation or a blessing for yourself.

You who live in the shelter of the
Most High, who abide in the shadow
of the Almighty, will say to the Lord, "My
refuge and my fortress; my God in whom
I trust."

For he will deliver you from the snare
of the fowler and from the deadly
pestilence; he will cover you with his pinions,
and under his wings you will find refuge;
his faithfulness is a shield and buckler.

You will not fear the terror of the
night, or the arrow that flies by day,
or the pestilence that stalks in darkness,
or the destruction that wastes at noonday.

Psalm 91: 1-6

12

Images of Comfort

ONCE I SAW GOD in a dream. As if that were not enough of a surprise, the form of God came as an even greater shock. I saw a large majestic bird circle slowly out of the sky and alight. It appeared a strong and powerful creature, something like a falcon but with feathers shimmering blue and green like a peacock's. A brilliant light silhouetted the bird from behind. I'm not sure how I knew this beautiful creature symbolized God, but I did know beyond a doubt.

After absorbing the disturbing message, I lay in bed reflecting on the form of God in my dream. God as a bird? Then I recalled the baptism of Jesus by John in the Jordan River. A gentle dove descended from heaven to declare Jesus as God's beloved Son (Matthew 3:16). When the people of Israel sojourned in the desert, God guided them as an eagle, hovering above its young, spreads its pinions and takes them up, carrying them upon eagle wings (Deuteronomy 32:11). Jesus laments over the wickedness of Jerusalem and longs to gather her children as a hen gathers her brood under her wings (Matthew 23:37). God—the wild, awesome bird who challenges! God—the snuggly, soft bird who comforts!

Psalm 91's images of God can bring solace to the sick and their caregivers. In the presence of illness, we feel vulnerable, fearful, powerless, weak. At just such times, we become most receptive to God's tender grace. God longs to provide refuge, security, comfort, peace. Reread Psalm 91:1-6. "The shelter of the Most High" is a figure of speech for protection given by God. We can call God our "refuge" and "fortress." Both words conjure up feelings of security. We may trust God to deliver us from dangers.

God's protection is compared to the care of a mother bird for her chicks. The mother covers us with her wings. We run to her when evil threatens. She hides us in safety as we snuggle against her downy breast. Her perseverance shields from the terrors of the night.

The psalm continues with a list representing all forms of threatening reality—sinister forces, demonic powers, evils real or imagined, diseases, enemies. From all threats we are safe and can rest, tranquil under the shadow of God's wings.

In times of serious illness we sometimes look everywhere for comfort but to God. Yet God remains close at hand, ready to restore those who trust. When we desire to stand in God's presence, then we are already there. God's presence requires only our desire. Ask nothing, expect nothing; just believe in God's love. Resting in God's love in silence is the deepest level of prayer. We simply abide in God's presence and enjoy one another's company. The Spirit intercedes for us. This is the prayer of the Spirit, a prayer too deep for words (Romans 8:26-27).

God invites us into this intimate, loving relationship. Flee your anxieties. Come as you are. Take refuge under God's protective wing and bask in divine love. The familiar hymn "Abide with Me" invites us to rest in God's presence.

ABIDE WITH ME

Abide with me; fast falls the eventide;
the darkness deepens; Lord, with me abide.
When other helpers fail and comforts flee,
Help of the helpless, O abide with me.

Swift to its close ebbs out life's little day;
earth's joys grow dim; its glories pass away;
change and decay in all around I see;
O Thou who changest not, abide with me.

I need thy presence every passing hour.
What but thy grace can foil the tempter's power?
Who, like thyself, my guide and stay can be?
Through cloud and sunshine, Lord, abide with me.

I fear no foe, with thee at hand to bless:
ills have no weight, and tears no bitterness.
Where is death's sting? Where, grave, thy victory?
I triumph still, if thou abide with me.

Hold Thou thy cross before my closing eyes;
shine through the gloom and point me to the skies.
Heaven's morning breaks, and earth's vain shadows flee;
in life, in death, O Lord, abide with me.

—Henry F. Lyte, 1847

For Group Discussion or Personal Reflection

1. Down the left side of a piece of paper list words that describe how you feel now as caregiver during your loved one's illness.

   Note: If done in the context of group discussion, the leader may list responses to questions 1 and 2 on newsprint or chalkboard.

2. Review Psalm 91:1-6 and circle words or phrases that describe what you desire from God. Do the words circled in Psalm 91 speak to your needs listed in question number 1? If so, list them opposite.

3. During this illness, what are your personal terrors? (Psalm 91:5-6) Describe the feelings. What has helped—or might help—counter your fears?

4. If you can imagine God as a bird, what kind would you choose? Is it comforting to think of yourself snuggled under the wing of God? Explain.

5. Do you think quietly resting in God's presence could be helpful during this current illness? If so, what would help you experience that rest?

6. Read the words of the hymn "Abide with Me." Which stanza is most meaningful to you now? Explain. Memorize the stanza and sing or repeat it during the days ahead.

7. Scripture poses many images of a comforting God, for example, God as a shepherd in Psalm 23. What picture of God, story, or teaching from the Bible do you find most comforting now?

   Option: Using art supplies, draw a picture or symbol of God comforting you.

A conversation between Jesus and
Mary Magdalene on the occasion
of his postresurrection appearance
to her in the garden:

Jesus said, "*Mary!*"

She turned to him and said,

"*Rabbuni!*"

(which is Hebrew for "My Master").

Jesus said,

"*Do not cling to me,*

for I have not yet ascended

to the Father."

John 20: 16–17, NEB

13

Letting Go

WHEN THE EXPERT on lymphomas at the University of Michigan Medical Center walked into the examining room where Dick and I awaited him, these words of Jesus to Mary popped into my mind: "Do not cling to me." I wanted to throw myself at this doctor's feet, entwine my arms around his legs and cry out, "Please help us!" After months of deteriorating health, tests, consultations, referrals, we finally had arrived at the site of the most expert diagnostic help available. Fortunately, I restrained my impulse and we civilly exchanged introductions and shook hands.

Frequently discussed by spiritual guides, clinging and letting go are more formally designated as *attachment* and *detachment*. *Detachment* is viewed as a spiritual discipline because it involves a struggle with our desire to control. It calls for an attitude of surrender and eventually forces us to acknowledge that our strength comes not from ourselves but from God. To sincerely proclaim, "In you, O Lord, I put my trust," is the supreme act of detachment from all else except God. It is the essence of faith.

In times of illness, for patient or caregivers, detachment can help restore health in a number of ways. Firstly, letting go can diminish distractions and provide clarity of purpose. Secondly, the process can remove hindering relationships and situations. Finally, detachment transforms a selfish, individualistic view of self to reliance upon God, thus opening us up to our real source of power and healing.

For example, when my husband became seriously ill, I let go in a number of significant ways:

1. I resigned as president of our county Humane Society, an organization I had founded two years earlier. That decision required relinquishing my reputation as an organizer and my desire to control the direction of the group. The decision also released me from the frustrations of being unable to "fix it" for the animals and from the stress of dealing with diverse factions on the board of directors. Running the Humane Society was a major distraction I could not handle at that point. I had to say to myself, *If it goes forward without me, it's OK. If it does not go forward without me, it's still OK.*

2. My husband told me one evening that due to a drop in stock market prices, we had lost money over the past few months. I did not even give it a second thought. During serious illness, material things became unimportant, and we let go of a sense of worth based on external measures.

3. My view of my husband and myself as capable, self-sufficient people was relinquished in the turmoil of illness. For the first time in our lives we felt terribly "needy." We knew nothing about Dick's disease, so we depended upon the expertise of medical professionals. We felt emotionally distressed and looked to family and friends for support. We needed prayers and spiritual guidance and turned to church members and our pastor. Instead of relying on ourselves, we were required to shift trust to others and rely on a new pattern of relationships beyond the two of us. The best image I know to describe the experience is this: You are going down a big highway and construction looms up ahead. A sign displays arrows pointing straight ahead; then the arrows shift direction to lead you around the obstruction; then the arrows point straight ahead again. The obstruction is the illness. In order to continue forward, a radical shift is required.

4. While Dick was in treatment, we received a letter from our local oncologist informing us he was moving to California. My impulse was to cling to this doctor also. I felt like crying out, "How can he

abandon us when we rely upon him for Dick's healing?" He was my security. I eventually saw that I had invested too much trust in him. The psalm in my daily reading counseled, "God will not abandon his people" (Psalm 94:14). The real healer was God, I realized, and a transfer to another oncologist would not prove disastrous.

5. I surrendered the assumption that Dick and I would live together on this earth forever. I began to think about our own mortality: Dick might die of this disease. He might not die of it now but maybe later. It may not happen this time, but it will sometime. Death may not come to him first but to me.

Dick is now finished with treatments, feeling good, and we hope progressing toward cure. His illness requires less of my time and attention. Our pastor asked me a thought-provoking question, "Will you be able to let go of the illness?" When healing of an illness results in cure, then we must let go of the illness, with its intellectual challenges, intensity of feelings, consuming purpose. During illness, life is not boring!

If the healing does not come as cure but rather in the form of death, however, the patient must let go of physical life. Those remaining let go of the loved one. If the one remaining is a spouse, he or she must give up a view of oneself as half of a couple. No other choices are possible. I realize that is a simplistic statement, easily put forth. The reality may invoke anger, doubts, questioning of God's power and love. The letting go may involve a slow grieving process over a long period. It may require participation in grief groups, counseling, spiritual direction. But detachment must eventually occur if emotional health is to continue.

The incident depicted in this chapter's opening scripture, when Mary Magdalene clings to Jesus, has relevance here. Jesus died and he then appeared to Mary. Her reaction was to grasp him joyfully. Perhaps she thought he had returned to stay with her and the other followers and resume their former relationship. But Jesus said she should not try to hold onto him. Jesus' permanent presence was not to be in bodily appearance but through a gift of the Spirit that could come only after he ascended. The presence of Jesus changed form. There is a time to cling and a time to let go!

Clinging and letting go produce tension throughout our lives. Marriage requires an abundance of both. In parenting we begin letting go the day the child is born. We let go of uncreative jobs, hurts over unkind words, harmful relationships. Holding is a form of care, but so is letting go.

Detachment, letting go, should never be chosen from a position of apathy or failure to resolve a situation. We ought not let go simply because we don't have the strength to hang on. We let go from a position of strength, not weakness. Detachment is an intentional surrender of a dimension of our being no longer life-giving for those concerned. It is undertaken in love, not selfishness.

Letting go within or at the end of life involves death of part of our old self. It will bring pain. Yet in the process we are not destroyed but purified and transformed into a more authentic self, the self created in the image of God.

> Lord, let me know my end and the number of my days;
> tell me how short my life is to be.
> I know you have made my days a mere span long,
> and my whole life is as nothing in your sight.
> A human being, however firm he stands,
>   is but a puff of wind,
> his life but a passing shadow;
> the riches he piles up are no more than vapour,
> and there is no knowing who will enjoy them.
>
> Now, Lord, what do I wait for?
> My hope is in you.
>
> —*Psalm 39:4-7* REB

For Group Discussion or Personal Reflection

1. Tell about a time when you gave up control of a situation. Did you do it from a position of strength or weakness? What was the long-term result?

2. During this current illness, what distractions have you given up to help yourself as caregiver? Do you think this letting go aids the healing process of your loved one? Are there distractions you still need to relinquish? What are they?

3. During this current illness, what relationship(s) have not proved helpful? Why might this be the case? Is it realistic to detach from relationships that are not helpful? If not, how might these be handled better?

4. What new relationships have proved helpful during this illness?

5. Have you let go of old views of your own mortality while confronting this illness? Have more helpful ideas replaced the old views? Explain.

6. Do you believe the process of letting go can lead to a deeper trust in God? Explain. Give examples from your own life or that of others.

Jesus replied...

In all truth
I tell you,
unless a wheat grain
falls into the earth
and dies,
it remains
only a single grain;
but if it dies
it yields a rich harvest.

John 12:24, NJB

14

Images of Hope

ALONE AT NIGHT with their sheep and goats, ancient nomadic shepherds observed the phases of the moon, from crescent to full and back again, and wondered about the rhythm of life and death. Farmers in eons past planted, watched growth, harvested, and questioned, "If a man dies, will he live again?" (Job 14:12). Observation of nature raised human hope for resurrection: "Maybe it will be like that for us too."

Birth—growth—death—rebirth (resurrection), these are primary themes in world religions. Belief in this endless cycle endures as an eternal truth. It refers not just to resurrection at the end of physical life but to all the smaller deaths and rebirths within human existence on earth.

We may picture life as spiraling forward. We are going along, feeling safe and secure. We experience contentment with our marriage, pride in our children, fulfillment in work, health and prosperity. These are the good times, and we wish they could last forever. However this up cycle is fairly boring and does not evoke great creativity. Intensity and passion seem missing.

Then comes the upset, a period of painful disorientation. The crisis may be divorce, loss of a job, move to different location, destructive behavior of a loved one, a challenge to deep beliefs, serious illness, or death. The old way of thinking and doing things comes unglued. Doubt, panic, and great pain may accompany this phase.

Darkness comes when we are forced to let go. We want to hang on but cannot. We are no longer in control. We feel fearful. In the moment when the old dies and the new has not yet begun, there may be a time of terror. "My God, my God, why have you forsaken me?" (Mark 15:34, also Psalm 22:1-22) We want to run away, but no choice remains except to continue on. We accept the pain and awfulness and feel like we are dying. It seems it will last forever, but of course, it won't. Within the death of the old lies the seed of hope for the new.

Both in this lifetime and at its end, we experience the rebirth as resurrection. The old has passed away and all things are becoming new. For those with serious illness, the new may be restoration of health, but in any event they will never return to their former ways. Illness has changed life's course. And for some who are ill, the new may be healing through death and resurrection to eternal life.

For loved ones remaining, the new may include a future without child, father, mother, or spouse. In the midst of darkness it seems peace never will revisit. But life falls into a pattern in unexpected ways. Wholeness returns in new forms, and we discover we can embrace the present.

Resurrection always brings surprises!

> It is the same too with the resurrection of
> the dead: what is sown is perishable, but what is
> raised is imperishable; what is sown is contemptible
> but what is raised is glorious: what is sown is weak,
> but what is raised is powerful; what is sown a
> natural body is raised a spiritual body.
>
> Death is swallowed up in victory. Death,
> where is your victory? Death, where is your sting?
>
> —*1 Corinthians 15:42-44, 54-55* NJB

O Love That Wilt Not Let Me Go

O Love that wilt not let me go,
I rest my weary soul in thee;
I give thee back the life I owe,
that in thine ocean depths its flow
may richer, fuller be.

O Light that followest all my way,
I yield my flickering torch to thee;
my heart restores its borrowed ray,
that in thy sunshine's blaze its day
may brighter, fairer be.

O Joy that seekest me through pain,
I cannot close my heart to thee;
I trace the rainbow thru the rain,
and feel the promise is not vain,
that morn shall tearless be.

O Cross that liftest up my head,
I dare not ask to fly from thee;
I lay in dust life's glory dead,
and from the ground there blossoms red
life that shall endless be.

—*George Matheson, 1882*

For Group Discussion or Personal Reflection

1. Tell about a dark period in your life. How did you feel? Was it like a death? How did you get through it? Who or what helped you move through that period?

2. Think about a "resurrection" you have experienced in your own

life and share that. How was the new life that resulted different from the old? Was it a surprise? Do you believe the new life was a gift from God? Explain.

3. What is one important idea you got from this chapter? How will it comfort you? How might it help you give hope to others in their dark periods?

4. Identify images of hope in the hymn "O Love That Wilt Not Let Me Go." Which one provides hope for you during this current illness? Memorize that stanza and recite or sing it during the coming days.

5. Because resurrection is a mystery, we look for symbols from nature to express our hope. A wheat seed is one example. What is another symbol of resurrection that carries meaning for you? (Think of Easter symbols perhaps.) What quality does the symbol embody that reminds you of resurrection?

   Option: Using art supplies, create your own symbol of resurrection.

Do you not know that all of us who have been baptized into Christ Jesus were baptized into his death? Therefore we have been buried with him by baptism into death, so that, just as Christ was raised from the dead by the glory of the Father, so we too might walk in newness of life. ❖

For if we have been united with him in a death like his, we will certainly be united with him in a resurrection like his. ❖

Romans 6:3-5

15

A Safe Place

IN THE CHILDHOOD game of hide-and-seek, players run off in all directions into unknown places where they try to hide from the one who is "It." While It is off looking somewhere else, a player may make a mad dash for a designated base and on reaching it yell "Safe!" That player can no longer get tagged. The whole object of the game is to get to safety. It seems to me life is something like the game of hide-and-seek. There are risks, impending dangers, fears, and then, flight to safe places.

Life brings relationships, jobs, even churches, that are not safe places. Serious illness does not feel like a safe spot either. Too much is uncharted, dark, disorienting. Too many comfortable assumptions come under assault. Too many transitions threaten at once. We desire to fly to a safe place, wherever that may be.

In scriptures, a metaphor for this experience of chaos frequently is water: cold, dark, mysterious waters. In early biblical times, the Hebrew people were oppressed as slaves in Egypt. Led by Moses, they made a dash for freedom to Canaan, the land designated as theirs by God. For them, that land promised to be a safe place. The Red Sea was their first obstacle, and God miraculously walked with them through it, the sea rushing back on its bed to drown the pursuing Egyptian army.

After years of wandering in a hostile wilderness, the people of God reached a second watery barrier, the Jordan River, the last obstacle to be surmounted before the promise could be fulfilled. Between their former world of servitude and deprivation and their future home flowing with milk and honey lay the waters of the Jordan River. According to the biblical account, the river ceased flowing, backed up, and the people walked between the waters on dry soil into the promised land (Joshua 3:15-17). Later, poets sang about how God had turned back the river at the approach of Israel (Psalm 114:3). God's active protection brought them through chaotic waters to their safe place and a time of new life.

In the Christian church, baptism symbolizes a similar experience. The waters are overcome, and the baptized person emerges victorious over the chaos of sin and death. Those baptized into Christ Jesus are baptized into his death, buried with him, and then raised to newness of life (see Romans 6:1-9). Baptism reenacts death and resurrection. I think total immersion into water ritualizes the story best. The person is plunged beneath the surface of the water into death, is momentarily buried, and then raised out of the water to symbolize resurrection to new life. Because Jesus walked through the waters of death to resurrection, we cherish the same hope. We are invited to participate in his experience.

For a baptized believer, the new life begins with the death of sin. Yet the death is not complete, and the old self asserts itself against the new. The cycle of death and resurrection continues throughout this lifetime, but we anticipate a time of completeness, when death will be totally defeated.

At a Roman Catholic funeral I attended, this connection between baptism and death was ritualized. The priest sprinkled water on the coffin and said, "In the waters of baptism _____ died with Christ and rose with him to new life. May he now share with him in eternal glory." A white pall was then placed over the coffin. White is the liturgical color for baptism, the color of the robes worn by new believers in the early church as they emerged from baptismal waters.

The writer of 1 Peter says the waters of the great prehistoric flood in the time of Noah prefigured the waters of baptism (1 Peter 3:18-22). The people who entered Noah's ark were saved from destruction in the waters. As God brought them safely through the floods, so we too will come through the chaotic waters to a safe place. The safe place may be a cure from the illness, but in some situations, the safe place may only be reached through physical death. Death may be the way God brings healing.

God's promise of safety for our loved one may not seem like much at first. We long for details of when, where, and how. To those named by God, however, I believe that promise can be enough. When living in the turmoil of an unsafe place, safety is immensely attractive. For the one departing, there is the joy of new life. To the one remaining will come the gift of peace.

> Do not fear, for I have redeemed you;
> I have called you by name,
>   you are mine.
> When you pass through the waters,
>   I will be with you;
> and through the rivers,
>   they shall not overwhelm you. ...
> For I am the Lord your God,
>   the Holy One of Israel.
>
> —*Isaiah 43:1, 2, 3*

DEEP RIVER

Deep river, my home is over Jordan.
Deep river, Lord, I want to cross over into campground.

Deep river, my home is over Jordan.
Deep river, Lord, I want to cross over into campground.

O don't you want to go to that gospel feast,
That promis'd land where all is peace?
Deep river, Lord, I want to cross over into campground.

> —*Traditional, African-American Spiritual*

For Group Discussion or Personal Reflection

1. Tell about a time, before your loved one's illness, when you felt you were not in a safe place. How did you make the transition from the unsafe to a safe place? Is walking through water a helpful image to explain that transition? Why or why not?

2. In the Christian tradition, beliefs about baptism have changed over the years to fit varying circumstances. Describe the ritual of baptism in your denomination. What is the role of water? What do you think is the core meaning of baptism as celebrated in your church?

3. Write one sentence summarizing the most important meaning for you now of Romans 6:2-11. Do the same for 1 Peter 3:19-22.

4. Healing and cure may not be the same. How do you feel about the suggestion that traveling through death to resurrection may be God's healing? Explain.

5. The hymn "Deep River" is an African-American spiritual. Many such songs exist, comparing slavery in early America to the slavery of the Hebrews in Egypt. How does the servitude of slavery compare with your situation as caregiver? How is it different? Describe your "promised land."

6. As caregiver for one with a life-threatening illness, do you feel you are in a safe place now? What would need to happen in order for you find some peace is this situation? What is one step you might take to help make that happen?

   Option: Using fingerpaints, create your own picture of a safe place, either for yourself or your ill loved one.

Praise for Healing through Death ~ from the Book of Revelation

A Reading
for use in family, support group, or other communal setting

Leader: **Look! [Jesus] is coming with the clouds; every eye will see him, even those who pierced him; and on his account all the tribes of the earth will wail. So it is to be. Amen.**

All: These words are trustworthy and true . . . See, I am coming soon; . . . I am the Alpha and the Omega, the first and the last, the beginning and the end.

Leader: **We give you thanks, Lord God Almighty, who are and who were, for you have taken your great power and begun to reign. The nations raged, but your wrath has come, and the time for judging the dead, for rewarding your servants, the prophets and saints, and all who fear your name, both small and great, and for destroying those who destroy the earth.**

All: See I am coming soon; . . . I am the Alpha and the Omega, the first and the last, the beginning and the end.

Leader: **Then I saw a new heaven and a new earth; for the first heaven and the first earth had passed away, and the sea was no more. And I saw the holy city, the new Jerusalem, coming down out of heaven from God, prepared as a bride adorned for her**

husband. And I heard a loud voice from the throne saying, "See, the home of God is among mortals. He will dwell with them as their God; and they will be his peoples, and God himself . . . will wipe every tear from their eyes. Death will be no more; mourning and crying and pain will be no more, for the first things have passed away."

All: Amen. Come, Lord Jesus! The grace of the Lord Jesus be with all the saints. Amen.

—Revelation 1:7; 22:6, 12-13, 11:17-18; 21:1-4; 22:20-21

ABOUT THE AUTHOR

NANCY REGENSBURGER lives in Vassar, Michigan, with her husband, Dick. She is a member of the Vassar Presbyterian Church.

Nancy worked for six years as a Christian educator in a United Methodist church. She holds a Master in Theological Studies (MTS) degree with a major in biblical studies from a Roman Catholic seminary and is certified as a spiritual director in that tradition. Nancy writes ecumenical curriculum materials as well as Presbyterian, United Methodist, and Roman Catholic materials.

Nancy is the mother of two married sons and four grandsons. She is active in environmental and animal rights issues. Her hobbies include gardening, cooking, reading.